Raj Doctor

ÁMAME Quiereme

A Collection of 65 poems
for
Messengers of LOVE

Raj Doctor is trained as an architect, town-planner and management expert.
He has worked with several international not-for-profit organizations.
Currently he lives in Jaipur. INDIA.

Also by
Raj Doctor

Fiction:
Melancholy of Innocence, Romantic Novel

Non-Fiction:
Ashtavakra – Dialogues with King Janak
NEUROSIS – A small BIG book
Un-Power – 65 Lessons to Real Empowerment
What is Human Rights?

Poems:
Potpourri of AMOUR – Melange (A-Z Series)
Smorgasbord of Eros – LOVE poems
Zen of Rumi- Non Rules of LOVE
Panoply of Ode – LOVE poems
Emollient of Valentine – LOVE poems
Passion Coloratura – LOVE poems
Ephemerals – LOVE poems
Pastiche Enamorado – LOVE poems
Peal of Romance – LOVE poems
Sphagnum Moss "love" – poems
Olio for Amoret –65 poems for a Beautiful Girl
ÁMAME Quiereme – Messenger of LOVE

ISBN: 9798462922121
Imprint: Independently published

This book has been assigned a CreateSpace ISBN

Printed and bound at **Kindle Direct Publishing**

Authored and Edited by: Raj Doctor

Font Calibri (Body) 8, 11, 16, 22

Dedicated to

ANGEL of LOVEz
Goddess Messenger

Contents

Fearless Virtueless Powerless Selfless 9
I YOUz We Us 11
Jeune Fille 14
Burning 16
DNA..17
Innocence 18
Wings In Flight 19
Footprints 20
SPUR 21
Quietus Ardor 22
From That Valentine to This 23
LOVE-Rz Embrace..24
Federated..25
Illuminator 26
Till When - Till Then... 27
Glimpse..28
Colorless Shroud 29
Honeymoon Bride..30
Prisons of Life..31
The Real POWER 32
Here We Are 33
DEEN 34
Mausoleum..35
Than 36
The Nightingale And The Mockingbird 37
Union 38
Teddy Bear Hugs & Kisses..39
Stamp Stomp 40

Atonement Gospeler's Escrow....41
Of Dying And Death....42
Eucharist....43
Alexander and Gymnosophists....45
SELF LOVE is a BIG Lie....47
Snowflake Thistledown....49
Without Anyone Knowing....51
Just Watch....52
Enjoy....53
Library of LOVEz Congress....54
The WONDER....56
Despair....58
SERENDIPITOUS....59
Aphrodite Venus....61
As Bright As....62
No One Can Escape....64
Homeostasis....67
Head-Start....69
Dehiscence Achene Seed....70
PRESENCE....72
Insatiable LOVEz....74
Go....76
Bittersweetly....80
Godz LOVE-Cosmos....82
Teetotaler to Boozehound....84
Rosaries of Infinite Ruefulness....87
Halcyon's Tranquility....89
LOVE Is The Only Awakening....90
LOVEz New Normal....93
Perennial TRUTH....95

Honey & Bee - Deseret 97
Ashamed Of Me 100
Sunbird's LOVEz Thrives 102
Theoros Axioma "Amour" I 104
Theoros Axioma "Amour" II 106
Fadista 108
Ever-Last 111
Good Better Best 113

This page is blank

Fearless Virtueless Powerless Selfless

As it's in the Nature
Of a stub-born Flower
We'll bud, bloom, blossom
We'll dry, wither & fall
We'll bear fruits & thorns

We'll combine all
Eight elements of Nature
Fire, Water, Earth, Air,
Nature, Ice, Light, Darkness.
In spirit of our LOVEz

We'll constitute beyond
Five elements of Senses
See, hear, smell, taste, touch
The spirit of our LOVEz

Swimming against the currents
Soaring against the wild-winds

We'll thread million galaxies
Into a needle of OURz LOVEz

It is in the void of the apex
That love's creation within womb
Plays the sounds of ONE-NESS

We'll bury our intelligence
We'll kill our EGO and
Carry our heads in our hand
To present a gift of LOVEz
Let the world watch -
What BELOVEDz-LOVERz do

To attain the joys of pain
We walk on the edge of death
We run on tight rope of life
We drown in the valley of fire
We slice/chop of limbs and
Sing - dance on water

That's how we'll eliminate
The chase of victory & fame
Greed of money & success

See how easy it is...
That's how simple it is...
To LOVEz each other

Loving me, Loving YOUz
LOVINGz each other

No sunshine - No moonlight
No day - No night
No black - No white
No dark - No light
No right- No wrong
No sadness - No joys
No truth - No lies

In the most trying times
And very difficult circumstances
We continue LOVING each other

The only state of being in LOVEz
Fearless - Virtueless -
Powerless - Selfless

***

I YOUz We Us

"I"

Since that day when
Our LOVE happened
I have felt blessed
I've laugh and longed
I've smiled and cried
In YOURz LOVE

Let the world know that
I too am LOVEDz by YOUz

My BELOVEDz...
Who has oceanic deep eyes
Cosmic illumination spirit
Wise, wisdom & intelligent
Brave, courageous & fearless
Beautiful, kind & compassionate
Caring, Empath & LOVING

Who whispers to me every moment
The words of inner-soul-LOVE
Making me crazy & mad in LOVE

Hey, World - Come and see
There comes my BELOVEDz
There comes my LOVERz
To meet me - To take me away
To save me - To heal my soul

###

"YOUz"

LOVERz - Come in my arms
Let me embrace you in my hugs
Look at the burden I carry
Of the longing in our LOVE

Now walk on my path of LOVEz
Listen to my LOVE-breathes
That only chants your name

My heart beats your LOVEz
It inhales your LOVE-feel

There is no one else here
Other than sweet you
Who LOVEz me so much
I promise you that I won't
Ever stop LOVING YOUz

###

"WE"

We used to meet everyday
We used to sit, talk & smile
And laugh together in LOVEz

Remember or not?
One day - without both
Of us knowing...
Our LOVE-souls got connected

We were illuminated by LOVEz
Our eyes told each other
YOU're the LOVE of my life

We were wings-in-flight
We were blessed with LOVEz
We were flying-soaring to heavens
Since then, we've always found
Ourselves "spiritually awake"

Now we are not shy to LOVE
Now we are not scared of LOVE
Yet every moment we still remain
Thirsty for each other's LOVEz

We remain each other's shadows
WE are each other's reflections
We were True LOVERz since ages
We are Pure LOVERz in this life
We'll be AGAPE LOVERz forever

###

"US:"

When we were young
We heard stories of
Immortal LOVEz
And we dreamt of such
TRUE, PURE, AGAPE LOVEz

Our dreamZ are fulfilled
The moment WE came into
Each other's LOVE-lives

Now we can not even think
Of LOVING anyone else
Other than each other

Everything in our lives
Feels " C O M P L E T E "

***

Jeune Fille

This is a positive poem
All professions are humane
Read it with empathy & compassion
Set your bias & prejudice aside
Keep an open mind while reading

####

I LOVE YOUz so much
That I do not mind
YOU naming me a "call-girl"

Let me be your whore
YOU can call me your prostitute
I don't even mind
Being your sex-worker

Pick me up as a streetwalker
I don't mind being your strumpet
Make me your night-day-escort

I will be your sex-slave
Your courtesan, concubine
Let me be your nymphet,
And your nautch-girl

But do not call me succubus
Because I like you being awake

Make me your femme fatale

Procure me from a brothel
Name me a harlot or tart

Let me be your paramour or
Your odalisque and doxy

I do not mind walking
Your street as a slattern

Call me slut, slag, low or
A trollop, bimbo, geisha

I just want to be
Your companion

Accept me as your only
Seductress and temptress

Make me your damsel "Jeune Fille"
I want to be your vestal virgin

Use me, abuse me, re-use me
Dis-use me, dump me, ditch me

And when I grow old for you
Dispose me, drown me, bury me

I LOVE YOU so much dearZ
That I do not mind anything

But let me show you
How much I LOVE YOU
It does not matter
What names you call me

Just allow me to
Show my LOVEz to YOU

***

Burning

Let this fire of BELOVEDz
Burn forever within me

Let the world appreciate
The silences of a LOVERz

I pray blessings on
The one who LOVEz me

The one who faces life
Alone burning in my LOVEz

****

DNA

Give me an abode
Under your skin

My body has left me
My mind is numb
My heart is yourZ

Let me flow
Through your veins
Like your blood

Let me be
Your oxygen
Make me your cell
A part of your DNA

****

Innocence

There's no
Other place
We can grow our
Flowers of LOVEz

In the
Ultimate
Union of
Our ONE-ness

Let my
Melancholy
And your
Creation
Give birth to our
Innocence

***

Wings In Flight

I've lost everything
I can call my own

I carry no baggage
I carry no burden
I do not even have
A will to live

I am fallen
Don't let me
Fall more

Hold me tight
Take me with YOUz
Wings in flight

****

Footprints

I'm sitting on the
Path of your life
Pick me up and
Cover me
With the blanket
Of your hugs

Touch me
Feather light
Kiss me
Deep delight

Lift me in your arms
Walk on the beach
Let me turn & see
Only your footprints
On the wet sand
Carrying me...!

***

SPUR

YOU give me space
Within YOU to
Bury my defeats

YOU consistently win
The battles of our lives

You kill the fears
And our doubts dies
Thus, our LOVE blooms

YOU shine your light
With your soul-connect
To let our LOVE spur

***

Quietus Ardor

I live the soothing
Darkness of your womb
May we drizzle earth fertile
Nurture & nourish our love

Let your waters seep
Deep into my subsurface

Let our blood flow
And soak our core
To plant our seeds

Hold me tight
Clasping light

Let our lives
Quietus Ardor
Meditate LOVEz

***

From That Valentine to This

From that Valentine to this

We carry the melancholic
Joyfulness within us of LOVE

With whom can I share
My LOVE longing apart
From you my LOVERz?

Yet much of my LOVE
I don't show - but that
Too is part of our LOVE

How is that every moment
YOU find a billion reasons
To continue LOVINGz me

From that Valentine to this..!

***

LOVE-Rz Embrace

I am so isolated
With life's success
I wish I was just
As simple as YOUz

Let us build the montage
Where my heart is
Seen within YOU-Rz
My being dwells in YOUz
YOUR soul breathes in me

I am saving all those
Precious treasures
Of our LOVEz dream
To share with YOUz

Life's dreamZ have
Distraught us
Otherwise we would be
In "LOVE-Rz embrace"

****

Federated

My "being" wishes to surrender
My existence to YOUz

Let me present my eyes for
YOUz to introspect within me

I am "myself" only because
Of your LOVE witnessing me

When YOU federated
Our LOVEz purpose
We became a beautiful
Story of born again

***

Illuminator

For your scrimp of attention
I gracefully gift-back LOVE

Your lightZ pierces
The depths of my
Dark abyss ocean
To drown me in fire

I glow under YOURz LOVE-flames
Being a dark shadow of your lamp

Now make me a burning candle
In the skies of your nightZ

When YOUz are with me
What else I need
Oh.. my IlluminatorZ!

****

Till When - Till Then...

Till when?

- Can our LOVE remain hidden?
- Our longing will last?
- The world will keep us apart?
- The LOVERz will be disgraced?
_ The faith/ belief will kill LOVE?
- The pride of life will humiliate LOVE?
- Will people amass weapons against LOVE?
- The world can pursue tyranny over LOVE?
- Others will not surrender power to LOVERz?

Till when?

Till then - we will "LOVE Love love"
And we'll celebrate, sing & dance..!

****

Glimpse

Give me the LOVEz of your heart
Keep me near your physical being

I'll grow a garden of color-flowers
To make our home smell potpourri

Through your existence flows nectar
Let me accede my ego in your LOVEz

I'll serve your self a lifetime
Just give a glimpse - my BELOVEDz

***

Colorless Shroud

I am a fresh
Fragrant garden of
Your inner being

Let my pulse become
Your rhythmic heart-beat
Bless me with immortal
Long-lasting Love

The colorless shroud
That Romeo-Zuliet wore
I pray for us - that shroud
To realize devotional LOVEz

****

Honeymoon Bride

In this beautiful world
Created by Nature
YOU are the ultimate
LOVERz experience
A BELOVEDz realization

What more one can say
Of the time and place
Where YOUR being exists

That's how I became
YOUR Honeymoon Bride
Adorn with flowers
Soaked in fragrance
I walk barefoot on
YOUR path of LOVEz

***

Prisons of Life

Only when
There is absolute union
Between two beings
LOVERz and BELOVEDz
Desires disappears
Passions dissolves
Into "ONE" Unison

At that moment
Nothing lacks in us
From the possibility
To liberate ourselves

LOVE brings much freedom
LOVE brings salvation from
Our own prisons of life

***

The Real POWER

When YOUz see...

- A blue lotus in a parched desert
- A sun shining in the dark of the night
- The stars sparkling on earth's surface
- An apple fall upwards towards the sky
- A forest without a single tree
- A language without any alphabets
- A life as an obscene illusion
- BELOVEDz reflection in your image
- And daily LOVE-letters for years

Then you realize and understand

- The real POWER of divine LOVEz

****

Here We Are

The one who
Kills us with love
We implore for
Their well-being

Such endearing is
The LOVEz longing
That only blessings
Are beseeched daily

If there are passions
Let desires be this
Instead of sad tears
Let benediction entreat

Who are those
That LOVEz someone
For a life time?

Here we are -
Living ETERNAL LOVEz

****

DEEN

Let the flame of LOVEz
Remain burning in life

Who is the FIREFLY of darkness?
Who'll risk everything and
Burn & die in love?

Who will annihilate oneself
Jumping in the valley of fire
To melt the Golden heart?

Only if one remain alive after love
Chase the life's sorrow tomorrow

In today's world of sin
Only LOVE is our "deen"

Deen: In Islam (urdu) it means Religion or Faith in word

****

Mausoleum

Since LOVE happened
Between Layla-Majnun
Tragedy struck their lives

Layla was married to
A Royal Prince and
Majnun lost everything
Work, Family, friends and
Became a mad wanderer

Through love-vibes/energies
Only Layla knew of what
Pain Majnun was going through

Their LOVE story ended well
Layla searched and met Majnun

Their mausoleum (tomb) is in
Anupgarh, Ganganagar, Rajasthan
Till date thousands attend
Annual Fair (mid-June) to seek
LOVE blessings from Layla-Majnun

***

Than

Imagination:
Stronger than knowledge
Myth:
Potent than history
Dreams:
Powerful than facts
Hope:
Triumphs over experience
Laughter:
Cures better than medicine
Wisdom:
Sharper than intelligence
Devotion:
Selfless than deliverance
Life:
Better than death

And LOVE:
Immortally "ETERNAL"
Better than life / living

***

The Nightingale And The Mockingbird

Our time together was
A very happy joyful time

YOU were the nightingale
And I was the mockingbird
OR were we vice-versa?

We celebrated our LOVEz
To our heartZ content
Thus we still LOVE each other
With bright sunshine in our heartZ

Without having any foolish ideas
Of ever stop LOVING each other
Now WE both -
The Nightingale and the Mockingbird
Sing in sync the songs of LOVEz

#happy #love #song #chat #message #meet #smiles

*****

Union

True pure agape LOVE
Is all intellect & emotions
All mind, heart, body
All eyes, ears, senses
All earth, water, sky
All ether, light, darkness
All anger, joys, desires
All trust, respect, truth, lies
All noise, silence and void
All religions, rights, wrongs
All virtues, moral, ethics
All this, All that,
All everything else
LOVE is all ENCOMPASSING
LOVE is the ALL - "ONE-ness"
That only BELOVEDz-LOVERz
Can witness in their UNION

***

Teddy Bear Hugs & Kisses

We live afar
Across mountains & rivers
Thousand miles away

We've made LOVEz promises
And we need to meet again

Wandering searching each other
We both have lost sanities
Being afflicted by pain-longing

If we don't meet each other
We will be in deep trouble

Come, let us meet in person
And take away all sadness

Let us collect feathers
Let us build wings
Let us wear gliders and
Generate some soaring winds
To fly into each other with
Teddy bear hugs & kisses

****

Stamp Stomp

Humans can possess only
As much as what is below
Their two feet on earth
They are standing on now

But humans have made their
Lives "busy"ness as fools
Work, travel, explore, invent
Destroy, exploit, kill & hog
Capture, accumulate & possess

Humans have been nuisance to
Themselves & the world around
Without realizing that in a
Miniscule life-time of 100 years
They will be dead & gone
Buried - eaten away by bugs & insects
Burned - turned into ash & smoke

Better live life & every second
By giving & receiving LOVEz..

LOVERz stamp their feet
BELOVEDz stomp their feet
Hoping humans will understand

***

Atonement Gospeler's Escrow

Let the whole world understand
Unspoken, unwritten prowess that
BELOVEDz-LOVERZ souls commit today

Through sparkles of teary-eyes
All their LOVE acts are served
For each other's good well-being

They voluntary surrender everything
To dedicate themselves perpetually
As a devotional worshiper of LOVEz

They subscribe only to each other's marrow
Signing the covenant with their own blood

It's their spontaneous act that
No law or commandment on earth
Can ever over-rule or over-turn

Enchase a maZar for them
Through their heartz UNION
As a plea unalterable & true

This ident blessed on this earth
At the feet of LOVE-Angelz altar

maZaR
The Uygur word is borrowed from Arabic
meaning "a place for visit" usually
Refers to the tomb in Islam

******

Of Dying And Death

Witnessing one's own slow
death everyday in LOVEz
And...
Witnessing others die:
- one we LOVEz and
- One who loves us
encountering death...

We realize how important
LOVE is compared to all
other things in the world

One can have everything:
family, friends, fans
work, business, colleagues
money, wealth, properties
but without LOVEz life is
"ZERO" a void of nothingness

It is in this witnessing
of dying and death one truly
Realizes value of "AGAPE LOVEz"

***

Eucharist

Those who LOVE are the
Real heirs of this heaven
Where euphemisms of life
Has no place to hide or rest

They who LOVE each other
Are the Queens & Kings
Of the whole universe

They are blessed when
LOVE happens to them

So they take a journey
And walk on a path that
Few have taken before

A path of suffering
Painful love-longing

Instead of craving for
Power, hierarchy & money
They live simple & basic

Instead of faking "strong"
They chose tears of LOVE

Instead of eye for an eye
They chose the other cheek

Instead of condemning others
They chose sacrificial LOVEz

Instead of throwing stones of
Hate, harm, hurt, humiliate
They chose to surrender at
The feet of BELOVEDz-LOVERz

They are the few chosen ones
Fated to choose LOVE over life

***

Alexander and Gymnosophists

Emperor Alexander met 9 Gymnosophists

Alexander asked Questions
(Inability to reply a question
Will result in beheading)
Gymnosophists replied all questions:

Q: Which is numerous
Living or dead?
A: Both doesn't exist

Q: Which breeds largest animals
Land or sea?
A: Sea is part of land

Q: Which is cleverest of all beasts?
A: The beast humans have not acquainted

Q: Which exists first
Day or Night?
A: A day was first - by one night

Q: How can humans become a
LOVERz-BELOVEDz?
A: When human doesn't possess power

Q: How can a human become God?
A: By doing that humans can not do

Q: Which is stronger: life or death
A: LOVE is stronger. Both are part of it

Q: The worst answer will die first.
Which answer was the worst?
A: Each answer was worst than the other

Q: (Undecided.. ponder) Ummm...?
A: Impossible question require
Impossible answers

For such witty and wise answers
Alexander pardoned all 9 Gymnosophists

***

SELF LOVE is a BIG Lie

SELF LOVE is for those who
Are with very low self-esteem

SELF LOVE pumps up false sense of
I, I'm, me, my, mine, myself - EGO

Psychologist who teach SELF-LOVE
Are ignorant & make the world
A club of zombie narcissists

Most people who say SELF-LOVE
They do not know "self"
They do not even know "LOVE"

SELF LOVE breeds greed & selfishness
Makes world a bad place to live in

Practicing Self LOVE is artificial
It is fake and hypocritical

Self LOVE is the worst character trait
Of those who are fallen pessimists

Remember that people who SELF LOVE
Always fake kindness, care, compassion

Wise and wisdom says that
On Judgment day the perilous
Times shall comes when humans
Will only LOVE themselves...
That would be end of humanity

Self LOVE won't allow pain on self
For us to flower, bloom & blossom
To the process of divine purification

Self LOVE won't allow us
To sacrifice & surrender
Our pride at the feet of others

SELF LOVE is about faking happiness
LOVING others is about eternal joys

Self LOVE won't allow us to be
Radha, Kabeer, Rumi & Meera

Self LOVE won't allow us to be
Zuliet, Romeo, Majnun & Laila

SELF LOVE won't allow us
To be BELOVEDz and LOVERz

***

Snowflake Thistledown

The cold snowflakes drops
A spine chilling shiver
With each memory of YOURz

YOU pipe-me-up with
An entire universal cosmos in
A life-time of Earth evolution

Surviving & alive in your LOVEz
Is a MIRACLE only YOU bless me

YOU float in my life like a
Fruit filled crate of coracles

YOU searched me out to heal me
Fought ingenious battles & wars
Defeated life & side-stepped fate

YOU are my BELOVEDz
My dutiful LOVERz
Basking over moments
I live in your LOVEz

YOU're a GREAT-soul from birth
One who has become my
Inner-core & outer-case

Your LOVEz footprints are found
All around where I live & swim
Like flowers coloring my tears

YOU're my fiery valley & indigo oceans
Carrying reconnaissance rainbow vision

YOU're the last living
Avuncular magicians of LOVE
Who has kept hidden the
Final tricks of LOVING me in
Reserve when we meet again

We know that the
Major wood forests of oaks
And the BLUE skies
Filled with dark clouds
Will pay tribute to our
ETERNAL AGAPE LOVEz

But for now - YOURz
LOVE always parachutes
Inside our heaRtZ nest like
Snowflake Thistledown

****

Without Anyone Knowing

LOVE has made
Both of us Dreamers

We are not living our life but
We are dissolving in each other

Our souls have become "ONE"

Our lives have stopped but
Our LOVEz are moving

When we LOVE - we move
When we live - we stop

This passion is such that
Let the heaRtZ take over

Silently, like thieves
Without anyone knowing
We are stealing
Each other's LOVEz

****

Just Watch

Just watch how the skies
Have opened for us to soar

Just watch how the sky is
Flowing like a river beneath us

Just watch the skies merging
Into the ocean of ONENESS

Just watch the rains
It is rising upwards
And the sky is drowning
Within a dewdrop

Just watch the Earth rolling
Above the sky's clouds

Just watch the Earth
Flying above the skies

All and everything happens
With the realization of LOVE

***

Enjoy

Let us meet each other
And forget about
The world we live in

Let us be together
And make our own world

Whenever You're with me
There are MIRACLES in nature
There is MAGIC everywhere
Our desires are unbound
And our passions unlimited

Let the world guess
What we are up to
When we meet in person

Who knows about the time cycle?
It flows like water & dries off
What if tomorrow never comes?

We should not miss
This "moment" of our LOVEz

The happiness is within our LOVE
We "together" become the world

Let us forget everything else
Let us "enjoy" our being in LOVEz

****

Library of LOVEz Congress

My BELOVEDz
YOUR every cell is
World's biggest Library

I have spent hours
Days & nights without end
Sitting and reading
Various volumes of YOURz
Encyclopedia Britannica's
Making infinite notes
Bibliographical details
In your APPRECIATION

Your each pore
Is a cell-cubicle of LOVE
Where I find refuge in
Storms, rains, snow & heat
Between the heaps of books
That I collect and read
In total rich amazement
I archive your DNA in me

I've spend so many hours in YOUR
Library pores of skin catalogues that
All barriers of our non-familiarity
Have disappeared with time & space

Now You've opened your
Special section of
HeaRtZ BOOKSHOP
Only for my reading
Twenty-four-by-seven
Three-sixty-five-days

There are no holidays
In our daily meetings
Between those parallel
Library stacks where
We wander aimlessly holding
Each other's hand-in-hand
Passing LOVEz notes
Through our eye's blink

By now all the
Books on LOVEz
In the library
Are read by us

My dear BELOVEDz
When are you conducting
Practical exams of
What we've learned here?

Lets look into each other's
Inner core-womb as
Experimental soul-mates
To create a practical exam of
Our ultimate UNION

Many researchers are
Eagerly waiting to write
Their doctoral thesis
On our LOVE practicals

But till then let us
LOVE, learn and practice
Within our existential
Library of LOVEz Congress

***

The WONDER

Before The Creator created
Air, rocks, earth, & rivers,
Oceans, valleys, rain & snow

The Creator presented YOUz

YOU carry within you flowers
Thus YOU smell so fragrant

YOU grow different fruits
Ripe all over YOU
No wonder - bees and bears
Flock around you to eat
Your sweet juicy pulp

We have seen million butterflies
Rise & fall - grow & end - Arches
From within YOU like rainbows

Sound becomes YOURz breathing
When the wind blows around YOU
Which creates soul-stirring music
That soothes all LOVE-birds

Without power and electricity
YOU sparkle from within to
Illuminate the fire-flies
Of LOVE just by a little gaze

Like golden deer you glide
Past us leaving your musk scent
For mortal LOVERz like us
To chase you FOREVER eternally

The skies lightens brighter
The flowers secrete sweetest honey
The Moon and Stars dances playfully
With your mere presence & being

YOU are really a WONDER of sorts
Most BEAUTIFUL creation of Nature

Many GEMS are hidden within YOU

NO wonder YOU offer a glimpse
To only those YOU APPRECIATE

YOU only share your wonder
To a few whom YOU Trust

No wonder...
YOU are "The WONDER"
That fades all the other
Seven wonders of the world

****

Despair

YOU are there and I am here
Yet I've submerged my soul in YOU
What a wicked twist of fate
That I am not able to be with YOU

Beyond head's intelligence
And beyond heart's emotions
In the infinite space between
Life's chaos and LOVEz serenity
We can only call LOVE our home

As long as we are alive
As long as we are breathing
We shan't forget each other
Let us promise each other
Never to desert each other

How will we ever endure
The second separation once
We've met each other now?

We surely can not bear & suffer
A second heart-break's despair

****

SERENDIPITOUS

You've opened the doors
Your light of lotus flower
Illuminating my life's forest

Granting freedom to me
From urban jungle matrix to
Look at your natural beauty

Your whispers are listened as
The last Gospel of LOVE-lores

Our every birth
Past, present, future
Are created by your
Echo of poetic visions

YOU are the dream of LOVERz
Waning and waxing crescent Moon
With a Venus star floating around

You're daughter of Paradise
Sprinkled sparkled with
Gold-dust divinity

YOU bridge the sky & earth
With rainbows of your colors

You're the morning's first dewdrop
You're the last flower of autumn

You're the golden globe
On both the horizons
I watch everyday
Morning and evening

YOU're serendipitous encounter
Of my secret garden of Eden

****

Aphrodite Venus

From so long I'm waiting
On your path of LOVEz

Looking far towards
Your oceanic waves from
My white deserts sands

Twirling under the scorching sun
Bathing in my own perspiration
Standing on the burning embers
Waiting for your clouds to fly and
Rain a few LOVE-dew-drops on me

BELOVEDz - YOU're
My Luna Moon
My Sol Sun
My Ideal Idol
My Aphrodite Venus

I stand in between
The streets of life
Gazing at the mirage
Oasis of your love

I am sold at a loss on life's
Platforms of human greed

It's only YOU who can own me

Who can save me from those
People who call me "names"

Who cannot even understand
Or comprehend the depth of
Our True Pure AGAPE LOVEz

As Bright As

Though wise humans know
In their end that the
Dark is as much "light"
As much LOVE is "right"

Because life's worth
Does fork NO LOVE's
Illuminating light

Good humans are born by
The first wave of loving &
Take their last breath by
The last wave by loving

All GREAT deeds look useless when
LOVE has not danced in our heart

Ignorant humans who chase life
And sing song of success with
Victories of fans, money & fame
Learn too late, that they have
Missed to LOVE on life's way

Oh.. walking dead humans who
Are living on fake joys, are
Cursed by life's gain & greed

Such humans don't find wisdom
Of the eternal spirits of cosmos

"As bright as...
LOVE & LOVING..!"

Only divine spirits who LOVE
Dwell into those oceanic eyes
Sleeping on BELOVEDz lap in gay

Looking at beautiful smiling face
Blessed by a serene LOVEz peace

During such times...
LOVE fights fiercely
The tears of longing
While LOVERz pray...

Do not go gentle
With your good life

Life will burn and
Drain at close of day

Don't flee, don't run
Rage, rage against
The dying of life by
Letting LOVE happen
When you are alive

****

No One Can Escape

LOVE can't be
Forced on anyone

No one can even force
One's own self to
"NOT TO LOVE"

Yet LOVE is FREELY
Available to us

LOVE does not have WILL
Yet LOVE exists within all

LOVE lurks everywhere
In & around all of us to
Enter our inner souls
Through our heartz cracks
And light us unknowingly

No one can ever
Create or destroy "LOVE"
Nor can one accept, give
And receive "LOVE"

LOVE energies are cosmic
Given, taken and felt
With instinct & intuition

It may seem LOVE is
Not needed or wanted
But still LOVE exists

LOVE is never sought
But still LOVE happens

Those who believe in God/dess
And those who are atheists
Both and "all" need LOVE

LOVE does not have
Any prerogatives

Intelligence, thoughts &
Head's knowhow deludes
Humans to believe in
Exclusive LOVE's right &
Privileges for individuals

That is a lie of life &
Falsehood of era we live in

LOVE can't be tricked into
Argued and / or out-smarted
By cunning, clever, shrewd
Devious ways and means

LOVE can't be coated with
Wine, sugar or vinegar
To be swallowed even as
A bitter medicinal pill

If LOVE is ever "chosen"
It is an artificial faux
Created from thin air
Just to show the world
Without a seed of LOVE

LOVE is a catalyst
That works on its own
As nature's seasons

Feel & realize LOVE that
FREES you from self EGO

LOVE was, is & will
Ever be & always exist
ETERNAL, INFINITE
UNCONDITIONAL AGAPE

In YOU, in me,
In us & everyone

Just like no one can
Escape the breathing
No one can escape LOVE

***

Homeostasis

Don't miss the LOVE
In the optics of - from
Where the words were
Written or spoken from

Don't check the brand & grain of
Paper used for LOVE-messages

Don't see which email
Provider was used for
Sending the LOVE-mail

Don't ask which route
Messenger took to come
And deliver LOVE-letters

Don't see the looks &
Dress of the messenger

LoveRZ and BELOVED are
Messengers of God's LOVE
And Both of them are
LOVEz Seed Dispersals

Please don't shoot the
Messengers of LOVEz

Just read the message
With all joyful ardor

Don't stop LOVEz kindle

The more one tries
To douse one's LOVE
More love burns bright

NO one has succeeded in
Killing one's own LOVE

NO one has succeeded
In killing someone
Else's TRUE LOVEz

Life sucks out goodness
But LOVE revitalizes
Nature's creatives & our
Birth's core homeostasis

***

Head-Start

I cut my darkness
With YOURz light

I try to remove
My broken roots
From life's soil

But somehow
Somewhere, something
Is left behind of
YOURz LOVE light
Inside me

Your illumination always
Remains nested in me

Your roots seeded
Deep within my soil
Should I say instead:
"Within my soul"

I am trying to get
Hold of my life to
Reciprocate your LOVEz

That is a decent sort
Of Head-Start
I make in YOURz LOVE

***

Dehiscence Achene Seed

Earlier I used to
Wander "wonder" endless

It was so confusing to
Lose my self to YOUz

But now I feel blessed to
Have lost myself in YOUz

I know I face
An aimless future
But the wander within
YOURz unknowns
Makes my life so
Worthy to live now

Not knowing what is
The next marvel you'll
Throw at me for exploring
It's wonderfully "WOW"

I witness my dusk and
Journeyed to your dawn
Every day and every night

Leaving my worldly self
- Far far away...
To explore the
Light and shade of
Your majestic "wajood"

Your INTELLIGENCE & BEAUTY
Captures my heart and soul
I fly WINGS-IN-FLIGHT to make
My dreamZ your fantasies

YOUz seem so near to me
Yet our UNION seems so far

Like breeze I buss
All over YOURz skin
From your East to west
From your North to south
Kissing each and every
Pore of your natural being

To seek the diamond cave
Behind the forest's waterfall

That's how you shyly
Present me YOURz
Dehiscence Achene Seed

****

PRESENCE

What is in life's appanage
Beyond the pale reflection
Of time-dimension's pain

One always comes back to
ONE's TRUE LOVEz of life

I think its the sound of
Your heart-beats that is
Pulling me to YOUz
To reclaim OURz LOVE

I am holding your SOUL
In my heartZ gold gild

Only "YOUz" can feel my
Heartbeats on your
LOVEz pulsate horologe

It is just a time-lapse
Between OURz LOVE-happening
And moments we LOVE-now

The sun, moon and stars
The gushes of breeze
The wavering oceans
The hurricane quakes

That rattles our bones
To seek each other
As our marrow screams
Calling our "PRESENCE"

YOURz mien consent is needed
"HERE and NOW" - OR when...!
When quintessence expires..?

****

Insatiable LOVEz

BELOVEDz - "YOUz"

The One who LOVEz me
Is beyond everything
What life has to offer

No wonder that your
Beauty gives complexes
To world's own glories

Your magical eyes speaks
Volumes only I can appraise

Let your cosmic sparkle
Glow-shine on my skin

Let your breath flow
Within my vascular

My finger moves over
Your Venus shaped
Lively statuesque

In your LOVE-making spree
I cross every boundary of
Being a risque honeymoon bride

To set ourselves in grooves
We broach our limbs out
Embarking our LOVE moves

Your fragrance is a MIRACLE
That gives birth to LOVEz
Abreast untouched orgasm

Wearing my heart on sleeve
Into YOUR being I discern
Seeding my implants clamp

Let our open lips get pampered
Let our primal happen unhampered

Let our reciprocity
Inject within us
The Lethal doses of
Insatiable LOVEz

"Close our eyes"
Let us submerge
Into each other

***

Go

AGONY

If you don't LOVE me
Go - Go - GO now..!

I've grieved in pain
So much in OURz LOVE
I suffer here and now
Go my BELOVEDz
Go my LOVERz
Go - Go.. GO...!

YOUz know that
I can't live alone
Without YOU for a second
But if you don't LOVE me
Go - Go - GO...!

Make a ZOMBIE of me
A dead person walking

Let only miles "Distance" us
But let our "Soul-Love Connect"

Sometimes, you give me grief
Sometimes happiness & dreams
Sometimes smiles & sadness
Sometimes despairs & joys

Why YOU play with me
Such Hide and Seek
Games of LOVEz?

Go - Go - GO...!
I cry in your longing..!

My Sweetheartz
Leave me to my fate -
Go- Go - GO...!

Every minute
I stayed away
From YOUz
I died every second

I want YOU to know that
Before YOU Go - Go - GO..,!

Search your dollars
Search your diamonds
Search your Sufi path
Search your BODHI TREE
Search your NIRVANA

I offered you all I've
In my LOVE for YOUz

I scorched in your LOVE
I burned my heart with
A smile on my face
To keep & see you happy...!

Because...
When my dreamZ
Stood shattered in shards
It was only YOUz who
Always came back & stood
By my side holding my hand
To give me hope and desires

My HONEY-dipped LOVEz
After knowing all these
If you still wish to leave
- Go, Go - GO...!

If YOUz can't perceive
How much I LOVE YOU
It is only my LOSS

When you go please
Leave no trace
Of our Eternal LOVEz
In me or YOUz

But remember to come back
To take my ashes and
Sprinkle near the bench
In the garden we planned
(With trees, shrubs, flowers
Birds, animals - dogs & cats)
We promise to make
Next to our cottage

(Twist in tale)

HOPE

Is there not a scope
To clock back time?

We are still alive
We can work this out

Remember together
We are always delight
Exploring each other
Every day and night

We are destined
To be each other's
BELOVEDz LOVERz

Let us wait one more day

Please - Be with me today
Tomorrow and day after
Till the end of time

Please do not Go..!

The Roller-Coaster Ride of Emotions
Filled with Passions of LOVEz
Can't imagine living a life without
YOURz LOVEz dear

****

Bittersweetly

Remember,
URANUS is not the
Reason for our LOVEz
Nor has BRAHMA been
Witness to our LOVEz

The seeds of apple
Eaten by ADAM & EVE
Are the cause of
OURz being in LOVEz

Both LOVERz - BELOVEDz
Born in "abandonment"
In the Garden of Eden
Grew in famine environs
Hungry for LOVEz & loving

We were blessed and
Fated, thus we met..
To let True LOVEz
Light up OURz souls from
Life's hell to Paradise

We kept OURz
Heart's doors open
To let our BELOVEDz
Become our LOVERz
By opening the gates
To our soul's wisdom

We let OURz
LOVE-soul-connect
Happen to make us
TWIN-SOUL-MATES

LOVE is NO forbidden fruit
Of tree of knowledge & life

Forget about all
Greek-Sufi Myths
Lets meditate on
OUR LOVEz reality
"BITTERSWEETLY"

***

Godz LOVE-Cosmos

This longing in our LOVEz
Is torturing both of us
There are no limits in
The pain we experience now

What's the use dreaming
And dancing in the rain
Every day and every night?
And making LOVE there-after
If all we do is fantasize..!?

Watching everything around
Feels like we are a "White-Hole"
And the whole galaxy and the
Planetary system revolving
Around True LOVERz sunshine

We can't bear the distance now
Between the Sun and the Shine

Like them- we are integral...!

We need each other
Like invisible shadows
To witness our milky-ways
Within our dark abyss

We can't bear the pain
Of the massive pits of
LOVEz gravity that pulls us
Within space-time dimensions

Our incredible dense centers
Of singular LOVE energy is
Collapsing within us now...!

We are trying our best for
Life's "Black-Hole" to absorb-in
All our LOVEz star-radiations

Beyond Einstein's relativity and
LOVE'z constellation reality
Let our life explode into an
Anastrophe SUPERNOVA creation

GODz LOVE-COSMOS...!

****

Teetotaler to Boozehound

I was a teetotaler
And I drank LOVEz..
From my BELOVEDz's eyes

In LOVE I can get
A little tipsy turvy
But do not worry much

Even if I get little moony
Remember not to falter much

If I am punch drunk in LOVE
Don't say a word to the world

Sing, dance and play...
Let me devour her LOVEz
Being squiffy by her eyes

I am so tippled
I can't rest now
Even eyes are refusing
To sleep at nightZ

Is the world seeing
My ebrious face
Am I whirling...?
Soaring in the skies
Catching Moonlight
Or wings in flight?

When the sun sets down
I become ONE - stoned
When the moon rises up
I become ONE - beery

I will write emails
I will write poetry
To her everyday & night
I'm full of blotto LOVEz

I surely want her to be mine
I want her to be
By my side - even if
I have crossed my slosh

Everything one wishes
In a LOVEz cocktail
Everything is poured
Into her chalice for me
To drink - tangy boozy

I will gaze at her eyes - timeless
With funny inebriated daze

Nappy soused kisses
Makes my knees weak
Within her soft breathing
I whisper "I LOVE YOU"

Take sips of red-wine
Let her lips lock-mine
To pour spirit of LOVE
To soak our soul tight
Imbiber tiddly LOVE

I am carouser boozehound
Oh.. I only drink her LOVEz
Squiffy, bibulous LOVEz..
Only from her eyes & heart

I became her LOVEz dipsomaniac
I flow into BELOVEDz goblet

I'm not in condition now to
Live a normal life anymore

Pitiful, Poor, Pathetic living
Holy, Endowed, Blessful LOVING

****

Rosaries of Infinite Ruefulness

LOVERz - BELOVEDz are
Best represented by
Daggers pierced in their Heart
Yet never wearied of LOVEz

Those in LOVE have
Sorrows in their lives
That is the key to
Being meditative, wise
And enlightened in LOVEz

Just like our...
Crucified Jesus Christ
Virgin Mother Mary are
LOVE symbols of Calvary

LOVERz - BELOVEDz are
Elegiac with tears in eyes
Bleeding drops of LOVE

LOVE is the only power that
Can softens every evil heart

Thus one-who-LOVEz pray
As an act of compassion
As an act of suffering
For each other's True LOVE

When LOVERz-BELOVEDz
Walked past walls of life
Into the lilies of Heavens
Passing the Gardens of Eden
Covered with glories
Of the sunrise dawn

The world sees the
Great light like death
In the eyes of both of them
Standing lonely & innocent
Dressed like sunset dusk

Both of them resemble
Regal Divine Majesty

Walking hand-in-hand
With smiles on their faces
Swords impaled in being
Daggers pierced in heart
Arrows riddled in soul

Carrying within their murmurs
Rosaries of Infinite ruefulness

Inspired by
Purple Heart God/dess of LOVEz

******

Halcyon's Tranquility

Whichever the season
Place, path & period
History, time & space

Give both of us grace
To imitate each other
Devout blessed-ness and
Pious Blissful-ness

Contemplating passions
Exploring craving desires
Living sensual fantasies

Grant us intercession to
Firmly cling to each other
Zynchronized through dance

In the galaxy of LOVERz lane
Somewhere in the milky-way
With each passing night & day

Thus we can live till the end
OURZ life and LOVEz
In Halcyon's tranquility

The Purple Prayer of LOVE

****

LOVE Is The Only Awakening

*Look at today's world
Full of Practicalist
Realist, Rationalist
Formalist, Functionalist
Positivist, Post-modernist
Progressive & Neo-Liberals*

*And look at what they have
Done for us since advent of
Industrial and Marketing Age*

*Industrial Age: (since 1750s)
They have exploited Mother Nature
To its fullest - mined & deforested*

*Marketing Age: (since 1950s)
They have made everything of Nature
As a product for GREEDY consumption*

*Not only the suprenatist
Has led humans to WARS and
Brought to us calamity like
Climate change & COVID (Corona)
Poverty and Hunger of
Unimaginable Scales*

*The Modern "MEN" has led us to
A Wholesale Ecological DISASTER*

*By the advent of Digital Age
Mother Earth is left with only
12-15 percent of its life-species
Since what was at the beginning
Of Agriculture Age (10,000 BC)*

Today - As of now, every day
150 + species are lost;
And half of humanity eats
Just one meal per day and
They go to sleep hungry

Why?
Because of these
Idealist, intelligent selfish
Wealthy Rich Philanthropist
Saviors of Planet Earth / World
Who know how to talk right things
Story-telling parroted SELF-HELP
Inspirational, motivational speakers
Who end up doing all the wrong things

Yet their evils are not punished
Because all laws are designed &
Made to protect their corruption

Today's education system produces such
Degraded samples of primitive idiots

No wonder that when we look
At them with disgust & dismay
They can't stand us & outcast us

Let us simply ask them -

"What good has your
Pragmatic Realism really done?
Have a closer look at
Your logic & intellect
And you will feel repelled &
Nauseated by your own deeds
That is filled with
Inequity injustice, hunger
Wars, pandemics and more"

Today's World - the way it functions
Is regressive, outdated, overplayed

Everyone is taught to make-believe
In this wholly exaggerated delusion
Of success, happiness, positivity
With dubious ideologue of
"Fake it till you make it"

Amidst all that how to explain them:
**LOVEz is the only AWAKENING*

****

LOVEz New Normal

If LOVEz blessing
Didn't happen to us....

The sun won't shine like this
Nor the morning be so bright

The Moon won't wane and wax
Nor Stars will sparkle lightz

The breeze won't feel cool
The clouds won't fly low

Mountains won't invite rain
Rain-drops won't swell big

Dew drops won't shine diamonds
The flowers won't sway & dance

The birds won't sing songs
The bees won't suck honey

Everything seems the same yet
Everything is so differently fresh

It's the same life and path
But when you hold my hand
The journey is rejuvenating

Same breathing happens but
Heart beats so fast because
We inhale-exhale LOVEz

It's the reason of LOVEz that
Whole world is so wonderful

Without OUR Eternal LOVEz
We won't feel so intoxicated
We won't be longing and
Desiring each other so much

May be we would had been living
But nothing like this amazing
Feel & experience of LOVING

Where would be such
LOVEz eco-system if
Our LOVEz narrative
Didn't happen to us?

To build this LOVELY
Architectural habitat
Where would be such
LOVEz environment?

There would be no one
So deep in LOVEz
If God hadn't blessed
LOVEz new normal on us

****

Perennial TRUTH

I am like a breeze
No one can hold me
If you want to catch me
Enamor my BELOVEDz

I am like rains
If you want to measure me
Drown into abyss of
My BELOVEDz ocean

I am like a sun
If you want my shine
Look & feel my
BELOVEDz illumination

I am like forest
If you want my woods
Be under my BELOVEDz foliage

I am like a bee
If you want honey from me
Nurture a flower like
My colorful BELOVEDz

That way - I am everything
That you'll find in Nature
I am present everywhere
But I'm alive & only live
Inside my BELOVEDz being

The whole world is my home
But my abode is my BELOVED

All are my family & friends but
My soul-mate is my BELOVED

I live in every heart yet it..
Only beat for my BELOVED

I will never leave
This world because
Eternally I'm in
LOVE with my BELOVEDz

And...
My BELOVEDz is aware of
This Perennial TRUTH

****

Honey & Bee - Deseret

Much before we met each other
We were ONE OF A KIND and
Then through fate's rhyme
We met each other in-time

YOU showered a glance
YOU brought me sunshine

YOU taught me to find
MAGIC in ordinary kind

YOU made me ROFL and
I became your smiles

YOU bestowed LOVEz on me
When I didn't know life...

YOU became a fragrant flower
To make me your honey bee &
I drowned into your honey pot

YOU blinked your eyelids
To flap your wings in flight
That granted divine blessing
You became my Angelz Kind

Your laughter sprinkled glitter
To turn my sad heart to cheer

YOUz melt my cold snow
Into raging LOVEz fire
Your deep ice cold cream
Became my hot buttery drink

Your trust in my abilities
Made me believe in myself
We look at future possibilities
In anything & everything we do

Your kindness and compassion
Fills my hearts with joy to
Make all our troubles go away

Your ability to give me
Unconditional true LOVE
Subscribes receipt of my
Exponential multifold LOVE

You pass on to me
YOUR spirit & soul
To make me be YOURz
ONE-soul-spirit-Angel

Whenever I am sad
When pain pierces heart
And my eyes get RED
When I lay down to die

You felt my vibes and
Got worried for my life
YOUz healed me with care
And I came back to life

Since that time onwards
YOU are my Moon & Stars
I became your illumination

You are my PEARL and
I'm your white shine

You are my cherry pie
I'm rosaceous plum fruit

You are my breeze
I am your cool feel

YOU are my COMFORT
I am your EASE

Hidden within our
Mysterious unknowns
Binaries of secrets
OURz paired-LOVEz blooms

No wonder- YOU and me
Have patiently survived
TESTS of loyalty & time

In our relationship space
We are more than two optics

We are "TWO OF A KIND"
Who will never PART

"Honey & Bee - Deseret"

***

Ashamed Of Me

I speak in the name of
True spirits of LOVEz
For sake of God/dess
For sake of NATURE
And to deal life as
Mother Earth imbibes

When facing the cruel world
Most TRUE LOVERz stash LOVE
Under heartz floorboards

Fearing LOVEz will be ridiculed
We're not strong to show LOVE

Still we live everyday to survive
So that we can keep our LOVE alive

That is how without LOVING
We carry within empty shacks
While living a fake happy life

Then the time comes to
Let Go of the LOVE we hold
Because LOVE lives beyond
Our individual's survival

Only when LOVE tries to
Lift its heart and
Sing, dance and play
Then there will be hope
For World Planet Earth

That's what I wanna do
I want to lift YOURz heart
Fill it with my pure LOVEz

And let you SWELL high
Like a TIMELESS BIRD
That flies wings in flight
To face life and the world
Free, liberated, independent

But today, I'm ashamed of me
That my LOVE wasn't adequate
And I was not good enough
To passionately LOVE YOUz
So to make YOUz fly back to
Find peace in my LOVEz-nest

****

Sunbird's LOVEz Thrives

The monsoon's first raindrop
Fell on the nectar sucking sunbird
And the sunbird flew in happiness
Singing folk songs of Rain-Gods

Every time it carries a raindrop
Stuck to its under-belly and
Drops those "pearls" on petals
A Gift of LOVERz to BELOVEDz
From SUNBIRDS to FLOWERz

Same drop trickles down the petal
And soaks in the grounds below
To spawn a new bud to nurture and
Become an inviting blossom flower

The nectar sucking sunbird can't see
Colors present all around in nature
Nor on the earth or dawn-dusk skies

Sunbird's eyes only witnesses the
Damsel amazing beautiful flower

For whom it sings & dances around
Echoing a prayer of total devotion
Even better than a musical elixir
Of a good-night lullaby song

That makes the flower intoxicated
And fall asleep to let the sunbird
Come closer to the flower's core &
Drink as much nectar as it desires

When the flower wakes up it feels
Rejuvenated, relaxed and light
With gentle feel of sunbirdz suck

It wonders and fantasizes about
Where the sunbird's kisses touched &
How much it drank from my core?
The flower twirl and sways happily

Sadly flower could not fly like sunbird
But wants to merge within the sunbird
In a UNION to become "ONE" soulmate

That is the time a rainbow
Transcends in their worlds
Arching from the deep blue sky

Making the flower sway
Itself with the gentle breeze
Nodding & inviting the sunbird
To come again to make LOVEz

The sunbird sitting on a stone
Feels the sway & fragrance of flower
And immediately flies to drink
Passionately a fresh bouts of nectar
From the open petals of flower's
Rich bushy whiskers aristatus

With such pure true real miraculous
LOVEz story of the flower & the sunbird
The wizardry called LOVEz thrives

Most common SUNBIRDS are Hummingbirds
Who are blessed with sugar rush and
Largely feed by sucking flower's nectar

Across the globe there are more than 146 species of sunbirds

Theoros Axioma "Amour" I

(Part ONE - 1 to 8 of 16)

1. PYTHAGOREAN THEOREM:
The spirit of ONE-soul
Is equal to spirts of
Two-LOVERz-beings ONE

2. ALGORITHM:
The power to which
Life must be changed
in order to raise
LOVEz opportunities

3. DERIVATIVES:
The vibe a LOVERz emits
With respect to the
Change in BELOVEDz

4. GRAVITATION:
Every cell a LOVERz attracts
In every other cell of BELOVEDz
With a force varying directly
To intensive passionate desires and
Inversely to the physical distance
Between a LOVERz and BELOVEDz

5. IMAGINARY REAL:
Exposure to complex attribute
Of life's learnings that
Can seem like a REAL LIFE
But in reality are just
Delusionary living till
LOVEz happens to us

6. EULER THEOREM:

The relationship among
Every feature of LOVEz
That is true between
Two individuals to make
Them a complete WHOLE

7. NORMAL DISTRIBUTION

The probability functions
Of everything one does
In LOVEz peaks max around
The center of ONENESS

8. WAVE EQUATION:

The fact that the LOVEz
Vibes are superimposed of
Incoming and outgoing
Feel of LOVERz and BELOVEDz
In a multi-dimensional space

(continued... 9 to 16)

LOVEz theorems are inspired from
Real scientific theories and laws
Which try to explain mathematical
Equations and formulas applicable
To our real world that have
Changed the ways of our daily living

*****

Theoros Axioma "Amour" II

(Part TWO - 9 to 16)

9. FOURIER TRANSFORM:
Inner transformation is
An important processing tool
Of LOVEz that decomposes life
Into LOVEz spirit within the
Existing time & space domains

10. NAVIER STOKES EQUATION:
A LOVE model to examine
Changes in the properties
of LOVERz- BELOVEDz during
Dynamic LOVEz interactions

11. MAXWELL'S EQUATION:
The electrical LOVEz
Energies and vibes from
BELOVEDz - LOVERz creates
A magnetic field to attract & create
A LOVEz-soul-connection

12. SECOND LAW OF THERMODYNAMICS::
Nature's LOVEz processes
Runs only in one sense
And in one direction
And are not reversible

13. RELATIVITY:

LOVEz energy emitted by
Those who LOVEz equals to
Their physically meeting and
The speed at which they
Illuminate each other's soul
Making their EGOs and self
Interchangeable and thus they
Seem different physically
YET they are ONE & the same..

14. INFORMATION THEORY:

The meta-physical study of
Quantification, storage and
Communications of all LOVEz
Signs, signals and symbols
LOVERz-BELOVEDz exchange

15. CHAOS THEORY:

An interdisciplinary framework
where within billions exposures
That happen in life - there is
An underlying pattern that
Leads to complex behavior
Governed by deterministic laws
That makes two people LOVEz
Each other which can never be proven

16. BLACK SCHOLES EQUATION:

It consist of LOVEz as
A risky affair and
Life as a riskless state
Between them there are
Various volatile variables
That comply in perfect harmony
With each other when LOVEz happens

(THE END - COMPLETE)

Fadista

Love is our longing
Love is our sadness
Our love exists here & now
In our loving each other
In our pain and sins
In our fires and ashes

There is nothing more to say
When we love someone so deep
Melancholy is all that remains
In the love that we share

Love is our punishment
Love is our awakening
Love is our retribution
Love is our awareness

We were born to love each other
We are living to love each other

So tell me about your love
Tell me about your yearning
Tell me about your sorrow
Tell me about your desires
Tell me about your fantasies

Tell me everything about
The way you love me
Love me, love me,
LOVE me, LOVEz me

The way you look at me
The way you make me feel
The way you keep me by your side
The way you cuddle me into YOUz
The ways you kiss all over me

Tell me all the ways that you
Want "me" to make love to you

Just the way we both
Want to be each other's
LOVERz - BELOVEDz

Our words in ballad cries for love
Our melodies in lyrics shed tears

The nights we crave for each other
But still we are not defeated souls
We live fully in Making LOVEz

So listen - I will tell you
The ways you make me feel
How much we love each other

Are not we both surprised
With the ways to our love?

How easy you are to love &
Give me such divine bliss...
Now being so far away from you
I know what sadness is
Now I know what melancholy is

You always take me to
The times of history
Next to your ocean
Where we first met &
Fell in deep LOVEz

It is so amazing that
Since then it's all
About OURz love

It had to happen there
At the place you were born
In the land and shores of
Maria'z Fado "FADISTA"

This poem is a Tribute to
Maria Severa Onofriana
(1820 1846 - Lisbon)
A Portuguese courtesan
Singer and Guitarist
The creator of Fadisto
(Melancholic melodies of LOVE)

****

Ever-Last

Life has created an illusion
Of making humans believe that
We are different, we are special
We have identities and labels
We are separate from each other

Last few millenniums of
Human dominance on nature
To grab power in name of
Religion, politics & business
And recently by democracy - has
Separated humans from nature &
Caged our SOUL-LOVE permanently

Humans are brainwashed to
Reciprocate only when one
Sees money, wealth & riches
Humans have become reductionist

Humans have forgotten to
Reciprocate to True Love

Humans have forgotten to
Save the seeds of love &
To share, give & plant it again
To flourish humanity & LOVEz

Nature works in cycles of
Giving, returns & reciprocity
Let Nature's cycle Ever-last

Imagine you are the Nature
Imagine you are the TREE
Imagine you are the branch
Imagine you are the leaf
Imagine you are the roots
Imagine you are the seeds
That falls down & grows
Into the flowering TREE
Giving fruits and shelter
Illuminating love Ever-last

We all need to wake up
To celebrate our ONENESS
To embrace blessing of love

We have to reclaim our
Earth, evolution, blessings,
Conscience & our conscious
Because we all are
Inter-connected with love

We are ONE world
We are ONE love
I''m YOU - YOU're me
OURz world is LOVE

Ever-Lasting LOVE"Rz"

****

Good Better Best

There lives my BELOVEDz
Who introduces me to LOVEz

Sprinkling loads of smiles
Calling the rain clouds
Blossoming the flowers
Secreting the honey
Buzzing the bees
Painting butterfly wings
Drizzling dazzling rains
Arching a double rainbow
Setting birds free to fly
Leaving cattle on grasslands
Becoming youth's aspirations
Dew drops that stick on leaves
Water streams gravitating to oceans
Greenish blue tinge of deep seas
Flock of birds flying high-in-sky
Yellow dry hay rolling on fields
Intricate designs of honey-comb
Echoing silences of the breeze
Cooling touch of the white snows
Blazing hot of the desert's sun
Blue, yellow, orange, red horizons

Every being longs, loves and wants
The illumination like my BELOVEDz
SOUL-love showering on others
The kindness & affection shown
Wisdoms of hymns-songs lyrics

Language is such a useless tool
To explain OURz soul-LOVE

So I survive on bond of LOVEz-thread
Entangled within the webs of Nature
Hoping, wishing and praying that:

Today in LOVE is good
Tomorrow in LOVE will be better
LOVEz future is the BEST...

One who introduces me to LOVEz
Lives inside me - every moment
I breathe, survive & sustain
Here lives my BELOVEDz

****

www.ingramcontent.com/pod-product-compliance
Lightning Source LLC
Chambersburg PA
CBHW051433150726
48000CB00005B/2085

* 9 7 9 8 4 6 2 9 2 2 1 2 1 *